I HATE TENNESSEE™
303 Reasons Why You Should, Too

Crane Hill
PUBLISHERS
BIRMINGHAM, ALABAMA
1995

I HATE™ TENNESSEE
303 Reasons Why You Should, Too

by Paul Finebaum

CRANE HILL
PUBLISHERS

Printed in the United States of America
Published by Crane Hill Publishers
First edition, first printing

Library of Congress Cataloging-in-Publication Data

Finebaum, Paul, 1955-
  I hate Tennessee : 303 reasons why you should, too / by Paul Finebaum. -- 1st ed.
    p.   cm.
  ISBN 1-881548-55-4
  1. Tennessee Volunteers (Football team)--Miscellanea. 2. University of Tennessee,
Knoxville--Football--Miscellanea. I. Title.
GV958.U586F45   1995
796.332'72'--dc20
                                                              95-34962
                                                                 CIP

10   9   8   7   6   5   4   3   2   1

I HATE TENNESSEE

I Hate Tennessee Because…

1. Some of the players found guilty in the recent telephone scam were actually phoning a 1-900 number requesting their favorite fantasy, which was: "Beating 'Bama."

2. The school has considered changing its fight song from "Rocky Top" to "Jailhouse Rock."

3. Usually, the biggest bone of contention when two UT graduates divorce is who gets to keep the trailer.

4. The median IQ of Knox County doubles every time the UT football team leaves town for a road game.

5. UT uniforms are so bright because they are washed every year in Tide.

6. The movie *Dumb and Dumber* was actually the story of Phil Fulmer's 1994 coaching philosophy against Alabama.

7. Smokey has to be tested monthly for AIDS.

8. Each incoming Tennessee freshman is assigned his own personal bail bondsman.

9. The fact that Neyland Stadium draws 97,000 a game just shows how stupid people are in East Tennessee.

10. And how little there is to do in Knoxville.

11. Doug Dickey is next in line for a brain transplant.

12. The only thing growing faster than the national debt is Bill Anderson's waistline.

13. In the dictionary, the definition of the word "redneck" is the executive committee of the UT alumni association.

14. The NCAA has moved a branch office to the UT campus to cut down on travel expenses.

15. The Knoxville police often borrow UT players for lineups to make the setting more realistic.

16. Forrest Gump chose Alabama over UT because he wanted an academic challenge.

17. The Knoxville campus doesn't need a Comedy Club. All the students have to do for a laugh is watch old films of the Alabama-Tennessee series.

18. Phil Fulmer can say less in more time than any human being in the world.

19. A tornado recently hit Knoxville and did $2 million worth of improvement.

20. UT has not won a national championship in four decades but has ranked high during that time in NCAA investigations.

21. The bumper sticker "Wait Until Next Year" has been the UT bookstore's best-seller every year on the third Monday in October.

22. John Majors' biography sold like wildfire. It was so bad everyone burned it.

23. Most Tennessee players were afraid to see the movie *Crimson Tide* because they thought they would get beaten up.

24. O.J. Simpson was recruited by UT but decided against going after they offered him a Mustang instead of a Ford Bronco.

25. *The Bubba Handbook* is issued to every student at freshmen orientation.

26. UT graduates get a free commercial fishing license with their diploma.

27. Phil Fulmer's uncle must have been the American lookout at Pearl Harbor.

28. UT graduates don't tell their kids the bedtime story *Three Little Bears* because it reminds them of Alabama and Bear Bryant.

29. UT folks honestly believe being a lawyer is an honorable profession since the school turns out so many.

30. The best thing you can say about the University of Tennessee is that it's not in Arkansas.

31. The most popular class last semester at UT: How to write on a bathroom wall in Pig Latin.

32. Lamar Alexander is living proof you don't need a three digit IQ to get a job at Tennessee.

33. Happiness is seeing Knoxville, Tennessee in your rearview mirror.

34. Phil Fulmer got the job at Tennessee because he was the only candidate that spelled his name right on the application.

35. John Ward is the kind of person who goes to an orgy and complains about the cheese dip.

36. Bug zappers with John Majors' picture on them are hot sellers this year in Knoxville.

37. UT basketball players can do practically everything with the ball but sign it.

38. Knoxville isn't the end of the world but you can sure see it from there.

39. Aunt Bee was once captain of the UT cheerleading squad.

40. Only 23 percent of UT fans have ever owned a bottle of mouthwash.

41. What is orange and white, 100 yards long, and has two front teeth? The front row at Neyland Stadium.

42. Some UT fans are boycotting Mount Rushmore next summer because General Neyland's face isn't featured.

43. *Gone With the Wind* is a famous movie about the South, but it's also what happens to most Vols fans' homes during a tornado.

44. Some UT fans think Dr. Pepper is the team doctor.

45. You can always tell when it's finals time at UT. That's when the football players buy the textbooks.

46. Guessing the "Final Jeopardy" answer is a requirement for admission to UT Law School.

47. It's hard to tell the difference between a Barbie Doll and a UT cheerleader—except the Barbie is less plastic.

48. The leaves begin to fall every autumn about the same time the UT football team does.

49. UT cheerleaders only have sex on days that end in a "y."

50. Kevin O'Neill was once asked if he ever talked to his wife during sex. "No," he answered, "but I do have her phone number."

51. Phil Fulmer would have been a Rhodes Scholar at UT if it hadn't been for his grades.

52. The television show *America's Most Wanted* was based on the UT football program.

53. UT has a rehabilitation hospital for students who are Hooked on Phonics.

54. Most UT graduates think O.J. Simpson is Bart's father.

55. A good season now at UT means not being investigated by the NCAA.

56. Some UT fans still light a candle every year on Batman's birthday.

57. Doug Dickey would be an ideal patient for Dr. Kevorkian.

58. UT has a graduate school for belching.

59. The only time Phil Fulmer has not tried to run up the score is when he took his ACT.

60. The No. 1 cologne used by UT players is Ben-Gay.

61. The FDA is considering using recordings of Phil Fulmer's television show to treat sleeping disorders.

62. Will Rogers obviously never met Doug Dickey.

63. Favorite pickup line of a UT player: "Didn't we almost flunk out together?"

64. The place to stay in Knoxville is the Roach Motel.

65. O.J. Simpson should have tried to escape to Knoxville because they would never have thought to look for a football player there.

66. There is a new course at UT titled, "How to turn on a VCR."

67. The notion that other schools are intimidated by playing at Neyland Stadium is a bigger joke than Bill Clinton's marriage to Hillary.

68. UT passes itself off as an academic institution when it is really nothing more than a football factory.

69. Peyton Manning was admitted to school by getting three letters of his first name and two of his second right on the application.

70. Smokey is the dumbest mascot in college sports.

71. General Neyland would roll over in his grave if he could see the coaches currently employed on campus.

72. The men at UT have so little understanding of pretty women that posters of "The Fabulous Sports Babe" are often seen on dorm room walls.

73. Since they are so popular, UT officials ought to consider putting steroid dispensers in the football locker room.

74. Bill Bates wrote his senior thesis at UT on the best way to keep a skunk from smelling. His solution: hold the skunk's nose.

75. The UT business school has a course in managing a 7-11.

76. Heath Shuler said he considered majoring in journalism at UT because he was bored with basket-weaving.

77. Someone once put it best when he said, "I know they bend the rules up there, but I was watching a game between Tennessee and Florida and they started the game with a burglar alarm."

78. UT broadcaster Mike Keith has been spotted downtown wearing a sign, "Will broadcast for food."

79. UT has a graduate course called "How to avoid marrying your next of kin."

80. UT also has a graduate course called "What to do if you have."

81. An academic All-American at UT is someone who goes to class once a semester.

82. Peyton Manning believes "Planet Reebok" is the planet right before Pluto.

83. Some UT history professors claim the book *War and Peace* was about the relationship between Phil Fulmer and John Majors.

84. Jerry Colquitt said the reason he didn't want to play for the CFL is that he didn't enjoy traveling overseas.

85. UT players wear Nike shoes on dates, hoping their girlfriends will say, "Just do it."

86. Phil Fulmer can say absolutely nothing and mean it.

87. Doug Dickey always has two seats in the athletic director's box. One for himself and one for his ego.

88. UT cheerleaders are tested weekly for makeup poisoning.

89. If sportswriter John Adams died during a football game, how would anyone know?

90. UT football players are not required to go the library before they graduate. However, they must learn how to spell it.

91. *The Odd Couple* was the real-life story of Fulmer and Majors.

92. UT fans think Armageddon is if the Vols ever beat Alabama.

93. Doug Dickey has a hard time making enemies at UT because his friends hate him so much.

94. John Ward has a Venus flytrap in his mouth because it is always open.

95. Neyland Stadium has to put in a new smoke detector every time the UT cheerleaders drop by because their perfume sets off the device.

96. The following is a list of the 10 most hated sportswriters by UT football fans: John Adams.

97. John Adams.

98. John Adams.

99. John Adams.

100. John Adams.

101. John Adams.

102. John Adams.

103. John Adams.

104. John Adams.

105. John Adams.

106. UT has a class for football players called "How to turn on the dishwasher."

107. Bubba Miller was UT's nomination for the academic All-American last year when he spelled his name correctly and got the date right.

108. Some school fans think "007" refers to the GPA of the UT football team.

109. Phil Fulmer is so cheap he deducts charitable contributions to the widow of an unknown soldier.

110. Fulmer is such an optimist he actually looked forward to getting married.

111. Knoxville is such a hick town the picture postcards are blank.

112. Gus Manning is so old that when he was a teenager, the Dead Sea was still alive.

113. Heath Shuler once said, "UT football is great because you get to bite, kick, scratch, fight, and get sweaty—and afterwards hug a blond."

114. President Joe Johnson's favorite drink is Rolaids and Perrier.

115. The hotels are so bad on the Knoxville strip that to get room service you have to dial 911.

116. Heath Shuler once said, "If we didn't have to go to class, this really would be a cool school."

117. During freshman orientation, the school has a course for athletes titled, "Brushing your teeth."

118. Counting to 500 is a requirement for the Rhodes Scholar candidates from UT.

119. The most feared words for any UT cheerleader are, "Sorry, honey, we just ran out of bacon and grits."

120. A romantic date for a UT coed is going to Cas Walker's.

121. Football players at UT must pass "How to walk your dog" before earning a degree.

122. Last year's homecoming queen was so ugly that when they took her to the top of the Hill, she was attacked by a plane.

123. After reading Phil Fulmer's autobiography, one critic wrote, "Once you put down one of his books, you can't pick it up again."

124. Bill Anderson is so dull he lights up a room when he leaves it.

125. There is something to be said for Doug Dickey and he is usually saying it.

126. Joey Buttafuoco has never missed a UT-Kentucky game.

127. After trailing at the half of the Florida game, Fulmer is reputed to have said, "If we lose, no matter what, I'll still love you and your mommas will still love you. But I can't make any promises about your girlfriends."

128. The movie *The Day the World Ended* is about UT's annual game with Alabama.

129. The only thing that could make the UT team happier than winning the national championship is if they made shoplifting legal.

130. Caning must be legal in Gainesville because the Vols get beaten every year they go there.

131. UT fans think a honeymoon is when two fans bare their buttocks toward a public building.

132. Some fans don't understand why they go to a dentist to get a crown and don't leave with one on their head.

133. Others believe a bong is not an instrument for drug use but the sound of two UT quarterbacks colliding.

134. John Majors once said, "A mind is a terrible thing to waste. So I am donating mine to Tennessee."

135. Some UT fans think a jock strap is a football player who's into S&M.

136. Some UT fans take their kids to McDonald's and actually look for the farm.

137. A number of UT fans presume the leading rusher each year is a sorority sister who rushed the most girls.

138. They think higher education is when students have classes on the top floor of Hodges Library.

139. Phil Fulmer still goes to Floyd the Barber for his monthly trim.

140. Bill Anderson once cracked open a bottle of champagne when he received a letter from Publisher's Clearing House saying he was a finalist for a million bucks.

141. Asked about manual labor in an economics class, James Stewart answered that he was a great Mexican leader.

142. A number of UT fans are convinced Gene Stallings is related to Saddam Hussein.

143. John Hinckley's favorite pastime, other than dreaming of Jodie Foster, is listening to old tapes of Lindsey Nelson doing UT football.

144. Alumni think a Rhodes Scholar is a student traveling down Cumberland Avenue.

145. Some followers of UT football think a Winnebago is a luxury car.

146. Doug Dickey fell in love with himself as a teen-ager. That way, he figured he wouldn't have any rivals.

147. Outside Neyland Stadium, a sign reads, "Bein' an idiot is no box of chocolates."

148. UT football players get their early morning workouts by fighting for the toy in the Lucky Charms box.

149. Doug Dickey is next on a waiting list for a charisma bypass.

150. Al Cowlings will be guest of honor next year at the UT spring game.

151. Anthropologists have asked to see x-rays of Phil Fulmer's skull for display at the National Museum.

152. Before declaring a major, freshmen at UT are also required to declare which is their favorite dancing raisin.

153. All freshmen must receive a passing grade in "Sandwich-making" before becoming sophomores.

154. Doug Dickey is such an egomaniac he often gets upset at funerals because he's not the corpse.

155. The UT coaching staff had to start separating Wives' Day and Girlfriends' Day because a couple of guys brought both.

156. Listening to Mike Keith talk about UT football is the latest cure for insomnia in the Volunteer state.

157. If Fulmer ever writes another book, a good idea for a title might be, *All the Different Ways I've Blown the Alabama Game.*

158. UT freshmen recently voted *The Price is Right* their favorite show because it reminds them so much of their recruitment.

159. The program *Let's Make a Deal* finished second.

160. Doug Dickey has a pinup of Fred Flintstone in his office.

161. UT's communications school has a class in hosting segments of the Consumer Shopping Network.

162. Some UT students believe the book *How the Grinch Stole Christmas* is about the Alabama-Tennessee series.

163. The UT homecoming queen was so ugly she wore a turtleneck to cover her flea collar.

164. When Doug Dickey is ill, he doesn't need x-rays. Everybody can see right through him.

165. Dickey's mouth is so big, he can whisper in his own ear.

166. Dickey has gotten so old that his mind has gone from passion to pension.

167. The video of the 1994 UT-Alabama game is not a big seller at the campus bookstore.

168. Bill Battle is to UT football what Barney Fife is to law enforcement.

169. For years Phil Fulmer was an unknown failure. Now he is a known failure.

170. Larry Woody has no prejudices. He hates everyone at Tennessee equally.

171. Some fans think the movie *Grumpy Old Men* is about the UT administration.

172. The best selling book in the UT campus store this winter will be *I hate Paul Finebaum.*

173. One of Dickey's favorite fantasies as a kid was being in a one-act play.

174. His favorite fantasy today is Alabama being given the death penalty by the NCAA.

175. Dickey's best joke ever is his record at the University of Florida.

176. The movie *Forrest Gump* was modeled after the boyhood of Doug Dickey.

177. Of all the songs ever recorded, the one Dickey hates the most is Simon & Garfunkel's "Sounds of Silence."

178. The only time Bill Anderson is ever speechless is when someone asks him the last time he skipped a meal.

179. When John Majors' doctor told him recently to eat more vegetables, he started putting two olives in every martini.

180. Bud Ford is so dull that when he goes to vote, they hand him an absentee ballot.

181. Phil Fulmer once told his wife, "I love you terribly." She said, "You sure do."

182. Asked once how his wife felt about his 18–hour days at UT, Fulmer replied: "I don't know. I don't see her that much."

183. The only reason UT won services to Peyton Manning was that Florida got to the youngster's home after the bidding was closed.

184. For his birthday, Fulmer's wife, Vicky, bought him the hot-selling book *The Pocket Guide to Better Sex* and told him to start reading.

185. The favorite whine in Tennessee, "Why can't we beat Alabama?"

186. What do Doug Dickey and Bill Clinton have in common? Both should be looking for a new job in 1996.

187. Al Gore will be teaching a mass communications course at UT titled, "The most ignorant things to say and do on national television."

188. Two words seldom heard in the state of Tennessee, "national champions."

189. Instead of the team of the decade, UT officials are considering putting togther the best players at every position that are now serving time in the state penitentary.

190. Vicky and Phil Fulmer have decided to take their vacation next spring on the Internet.

191. Gary Lundy of the *Knoxville News-Sentinel* is fond of saying, "I have no prejudices. I hate everyone equally."

192. Kevin O'Neill checked into a Knoxville mental hospital last winter complaining of "March Madness."

193. Doug Dickey once said that marriage is the only war in which you sleep with the enemy.

194. Dickey also once said, "My wife always complained about not having outside interests, so I bought her a weed–cutter."

195. Some UT coeds are so ugly that local restaurants hand them doggie bags before they eat.

196. The only good thing about Knoxville is that it's close to the Smokey Mountains.

197. John Ward has such a large ego he bows when it thunders.

198. UT graduates keep their diplomas in their rear windows so they'll be eligible for handicap parking.

199. UT requires a 20 on the ACT for admission for football players and a 16 on the IQ.

200. UT has a special course for teaching the vice presidents since Spiro Agnew.

201. If UT graduates could read they certainly wouldn't like Gary Lundy.

202. For an athlete to receive a degree from UT, he must be able to write his name, age, and social security number without making more than three mistakes.

203. The reason UT fans look so upset at graduation is they now have to learn to spell the name of another city.

204. Charles Barkley considered going to UT until he found out the town only had one Pizza Hut near campus.

205. It is now mandatory for UT coeds to shave under their arms between April and June.

206. UT fans order *Sports Illustrated* for the free phone instead of for the swimsuit issue.

207. UT fans believe the New York Stock Exchange is when a group of Northerners gets together to swap cows and pigs.

208. Some UT graduates thought the 1991 Gulf War was fought in Tampa Bay.

209. Brian Kato Kaelin was once a male cheerleader at Tennessee.

210. Doug Dickey has a poster of Lisa Marie Presley and Michael Jackson on his bedroom wall.

211. Phil Fulmer once said on his radio show that safe sex can only be practiced on top of a bank safe.

212. John Ward once coined the phrase, "I was born at night. But it wasn't last night."

213. UT students can't understand why the show *Get Smart* is shown so often at freshman orientation.

214. UT fans were surprised to learn that the movie *From Here to Eternity* was about Pearl Harbor and not about trying to cope with Doug Dickey.

215. UT fans still light candles every year on Lassie's birthday.

216. Heath Shuler once said racquetball was his favorite sport at UT. "I played yesterday for three hours and didn't lose a single ball."

217. Phil Fulmer yelled at his team during halftime of the Alabama game, "What's wrong with you guys? You're playing like a bunch of amateurs."

218. Some UT coeds think intercourse is the time off between classes.

219. UT fans know the four seasons so well: football, football recruiting, cheating, and cheating some more.

220. Doug Dickey's brain is always fresh, he's never used it.

221. UT has toughened its entrance requirements. They now require you to type your name on the form.

222. John Majors has a new book coming out next fall: *The 100 Biggest Games I Choked In.*

223. The Knoxville airport would make a nice nuclear waste dump.

224. UT's liberal arts school requires a foreign language for in-state students: English.

225. Phil Fulmer's idea of Armageddon is being stuck on a desert island with David Climer and Gary Lundy.

226. The tour guide for the city of Knoxville is the loneliest job in town.

227. Fulmer once told his staff, "I gave the sexual performance of my life last night. I'm just sorry my wife wasn't awake to see it."

228. The following are 10 phrases that many UT football players come to know well: Big House.

229. Joint.

230. Life without parole.

231. Making liscense plates.

232. Bend over and pick up the soap.

233. The chamber.

234. Chain gangs.

235. "No warden, I wouldn't mind killing your wife in exchange for some time in the yard."

236. "No, I've never done that before.

237. "I'll trade you cigarettes for my national championship ring."

238. Marcia Clark masks are hot items at the campus bookstore.

239. Mike Hammond once told a date, "Love at first sight saves a lot of time."

240. Hammond also said, "If you think looks improve with the years, try attending a class reunion."

241. Dickey often contradicts himself—and he is usually right.

242. Some UT seniors went ahead and enlisted last year instead of waiting for NFL draft day.

243. UT gives a freshman class in remedial sex.

244. John Majors has willed his head to science. They are going to use it for an experimental rock garden.

245. Dr. Joe Johnson should be the UT mascot.

246. Bill Anderson once said, "The best thing about football is that it only takes four quarters to finish a fifth."

247. Knoxville is such a hick town the town hooker has to stand under a flashlight.

248. Doug Dickey was so ugly at birth, his mother was arrested for littering.

249. Dickey was so ugly at birth, his doctor slapped his mother.

250. Dickey was so ugly at birth, his mother breast fed him with a straw.

251. UT players are tested for distemper twice a month.

252. Heath Shuler once said his fondest memory of Tennessee was leaving it.

253. Wade Houston still can't understand why the basketball arena wasn't named after him.

254. The captain of the UT cheerleading squad has a 40 inch bust and an IQ to match.

255. Doug Dickey thinks the movie *It's a Wonderful Life* is about him.

256. UT cheerleaders don't like to lie out in the summer because the heat might melt their plastic surgery.

257. If a national championship were awarded for having the drunkest fans, UT would retire the trophy.

258. As well as for having the most obnoxious fans.

259. Haywood Harris has a secret fetish for Betty Crocker.

260. Vicky Fulmer once said, "People always ask me to speak about various topics. I always promise I will speak about sex and marriage, but being Phil's wife, I don't know anything about either."

261. Bo Jackson considered Tennessee over Auburn until he heard they were already over the salary cap.

262. John Majors left UT after several years complaining of illness and fatigue. The fans were sick and tired of him.

263. Ed Boling is believed to have said, "Our society doesn't need to get rid of our coaches. Instead, we need to find a way to get rid of the alumni."

264. Beano Cook once said, "Some people hate Doug Dickey like poison. I just hate him regular."

265. Fulmer often wears a cap during a game so no one can see his brain at sleep.

266. The UT cheerleaders have a Fax-on-Demand service on Tuesdays and a Sex-on-Demand service on Fridays.

267. The captain of the cheerleading squad is determined by which girl has the smallest fever blister.

268. Gus Manning used to think Captain D discovered seafood on one of his voyages.

269. Some UT fans still light candles on Winnie the Pooh's birthday.

270. David Cutliffe believes cellular phones are normal phones with cellophane wrapped around them.

271. Doug Dickey is a born–again cretin.

272. Haywood Harris is so old he handled public relations for Lewis & Clark's expedition.

273. Harris also quit gambling after the Civil War. He had the South plus the points.

274. Fulmer has instituted a "Don't ask, don't tell" policy among recruits.

275. Gus Manning looks so old it looks like he gave the pallbearers the slip.

276. Knoxville is such a conservative town it once banned Flash Gordon. The mayor didn't like what he was flashing.

277. The food in some campus restaurants is so bad the only card they take is Blue Cross.

278. Fulmer once said, "Suicide is the last thing a person should do."

279. Fulmer comes from a sex-crazed family. His grandfather died at a hundred and four. He was shot by a jealous husband.

280. The captain of the UT cheerleading squad made the band in high school.

281. She also made the football team and basketball team.

282. Phil Fulmer likes to tell the story, "My wife is always late. She was an hour late for the honeymoon so I had to start by myself."

283. Success hasn't gone to John Ward's head. Just to his mouth.

284. Bill Anderson was such a loner as a kid, he had to put a lamb chop around his neck to get the dog to play with him.

285. Some UT coeds are so fat they have unlisted dress sizes.

286. Flying out of Knoxville is so dangerous, the longest line in the airport is at the flight insurance machine.

287. John Ward has not smiled since the day his doctor told him he can only have one mouth.

288. When Doug Dickey was asked recently about the abortion bill, he responded, "Well, the first thing we should do is pay it."

289. Dickey is so cheap, he had baggies sewn in his pockets so he could take soup home from the restaurant.

290. Doug Dickey was once dropped as a member of the human race.

291. Dickey once said to a friend, "My wife is something. She has cut me down to sex twice a week." His friend said, "Don't feel bad. I know a guy she cut out completely."

292. Bill Anderson is so dull he could be the poster boy for brown.

293. Anderson is so dull he doesn't shoot the breeze. He kills it.

294. Fulmer said he hates sex in the movies. He tried it once and the seat folded on him.

295. Some UT cheerleaders are so ugly they are often mistaken for circus animals.

296. Some of the cheerleaders were said to be uglier than sin. That was, until sin sued.

297. One UT recruit got his red BMW the hard way. He had to buy it.

298. The campus bar at UT passed a new law forbidding school cheerleaders from opening beer bottles with their teeth.

299. John Ward is so conceited his head has its own zip code.

300. Fulmer often tells his players, "People who live in glass houses don't have much of a sex life."

301. Dickey is in a class by himself or should we say a lack of class all by himself.

302. They gave Dickey an unlimited budget when he got to UT and he exceeded it.

303. After five games last season, Doug Dickey said, "If lessons are learned in defeat, as they say, our team is really getting a great education."